Forty-Nine Poems

by

W. H. Davies

"The Kingfisher"

Forty-Nine Poems

by

W. H. Davies

Selected and Illustrated by

Jacynth Parsons

LONDON
THE MEDICI SOCIETY
MCMXXVIII

The Medici Society Ltd.,
London, Liverpool, Bournemouth,
Harrogate and Torquay

Printed in England

PREFACE BY W. H. DAVIES

My first acquaintance with this young artist was when she was two or three years old, and a bundle of mischief. There is a photograph in existence, even to this day, where this child is seen sitting on my knee in a garden, holding aloft in triumph my pipe, which she has at last succeeded in wrenching from my hand. Since those days she has grown considerably and, if we were photographed together now, it would be evident that my knee would no longer stand the strain. But she is still in her childhood, though her ambition now is to take the laurels from my brow and weave into them a few leaves of her own; and I believe she has done this with as much success as when she stole my pipe.

Mr. W. B. Yeats, in his preface to Jacynth Parsons' illustrations to Blake's "Songs of Innocence," says that he has not sufficient knowledge as an Art critic to do his job thoroughly. All I can do is to say the same, and leave the matter to others. But although I have no idea how any particular poem should be illustrated, I still have an instinct that tells me when that poem does not receive proper treatment. For instance, I remember on one occasion when a well-known artist, who had an idea of illustrating some of my poems, gave me an awful shock at the very beginning. His first drawing was for a poem of two robins fighting, mother and son, for the right to occupy my garden. "This," said the well-known artist, "is to be treated as a survival of the fittest. For that reason, I am not drawing two birds fighting—which could be done by any common artist who has no ideas of his own; I am doing something more striking and original."

Hearing this, I was deeply interested, and eager to see what he had done. But when I saw the drawing, I was astounded and speechless. For what did I see?

I saw a big, strapping young hussy standing over a poor old, bald-headed man of ninety, in the act of braining him with an axe! It was quite obvious to me at once that this was not the proper illustration to my poem. For instance, the two birds fought on almost an equal footing, and it was not always that the younger bird prevailed in the end. Sometimes the older bird, having more courage and more experience in fighting, was more than a match for the younger bird's extra breath and stamina. But in this drawing—what chance did this frail, doddering, bald-headed old man of ninety have against a stalwart young hussy with an axe: with her arm as big as a man's thigh, and a thigh as big as his waist!

The best compliment I can pay this young artist is to say that she has "got into my skin," and many a clever man has failed to do that. One man parodies my work and, when he makes a Blackbird say, "Good morning, Mr. Davies," is praised for his cleverness. As though any Blackbird would call me by any other name than plain Will Davies.

Another writer says that all my gospel of content is found in "A cup of tea in a country cottage." This again is called "getting into the author's skin." But if he had had the least knowledge of me or my work, would he not have said "A pint of ale in a wayside inn"?

But this young artist is more serious in her efforts, and has a better and truer understanding of my work. Not only that but, with all the confidence of her young years, she has taken nearly all my best lyrics for her drawings, and scorns to take any advantage of my weaknesses, for which I am very grateful.

In writing this Preface, I have been able to say a lot about myself. My little friend, the artist, is now welcome to all the praise and encouragement she can get, which I think she will thoroughly deserve.

August, 1928.   W. H. DAVIES.

CONTENTS

CONTENTS—*continued*

DAYS TOO SHORT

When Primroses are out in Spring,
*   And small, blue violets come between ;*
*   When merry birds sing on boughs green,*
And rills, as soon as born, must sing ;

When butterflies will make side-leaps,
*   As though escaped from Nature's hand*
*   Ere perfect quite ; and bees will stand*
Upon their heads in fragrant deeps ;

When small clouds are so silvery white
*   Each seems a broken rimmèd moon—*
*   When such things are, this world too soon,*
For me doth wear the veil of Night.

THE KINGFISHER

It was the Rainbow gave thee birth,
    And left thee all her lovely hues;
And, as her mother's name was Tears,
    So runs it in thy blood to choose
For haunts the lonely pools, and keep
In company with trees that weep.

Go you and, with such glorious hues,
    Live with proud Peacocks in green parks;
On lawns as smooth as shining glass,
    Let every feather show its mark;
Get thee on boughs and clap thy wings
Before the windows of proud kings.

Nay, lovely Bird, thou art not vain;
    Thou hast no proud ambitious mind;
I also love a quiet place
    That's green, away from all mankind;
A lonely pool, and let a tree
Sigh with her bosom over me.

RICH DAYS

Welcome to you rich Autumn days,
  Ere comes the cold leaf picking wind ;
When golden stooks are seen in fields,
  All standing arm in arm entwined ;
And gallons of sweet cider seen
On trees in apples red and green.

With mellow pears that cheat our teeth,
  Which melt that tongues may suck them in ;
With blue-black damsons, yellow plums,
  Now sweet and soft from stone to skin ;
And woodnuts rich, to make us go
Into the loneliest lanes we know.

WINTER FIRE

How bleak and cold the air is now—
    The Sun has never left his bed:
He has a thick grey blanket pulled
    All over his shoulders and head.

Big birds that only have one cry,
    And little birds with perfect songs,
Are silent all, and work their wings
    Much faster than they work their tongues.

I'll turn that black-faced nigger, Coal,
    Into an Indian painted red;
And let him dance and fire wild shots
    Into the chimney overhead.

THE WHITE CASCADE

What happy mortal sees that mountain now,
The white cascade that's shining on its brow ;

The white cascade that's both a bird and star,
That has a ten mile voice and shines as far ?

Though I may never leave this land again,
Yet every spring my mind must cross the main

To hear and see that water-bird and star
That on the mountain sings and shines so far.

THE EXAMPLE

Here's an example from
    A Butterfly;
That on a rough, hard rock
    Happy can lie;
Friendless and all alone
    On this unsweetened stone.

Now let my bed be hard,
    No care take I;
I'll make my joy like this
    Small Butterfly;
Whose happy heart has power
    To make a stone a flower.

MY LOVE COULD WALK

My Love could walk in richer hues
    Than any bird of paradise,
And no one envy her her dress :
    Since in her looks the world would see
A robin's love and friendliness.

And she could be the lily fair,
    More richly dressed than all her kind,
And no one envy her her gain,
    Since in her looks the world would see
A daisy that was sweet and plain.

Oh, she could sit like any queen
    That's nailed by diamonds to a throne,
Her splendour envied by not one :
    Since in her looks the world would see
A queen that's more than half a nun.

JENNY WREN

Her sight is short, she comes
      quite near ;
A foot to me's a mile to her ;
And she is known as Jenny Wren,
The smallest bird in England. When
I heard that little bird at first,
Methought her frame would surely burst
With earnest song.   Oft had I seen
Her running under leaves so green,
Or in the grass when fresh and wet,
As though her wings she would forget.
And, seeing this, I said to her—
" My pretty runner, you prefer
To be a thing to run unheard
Through leaves and grass, and not a bird ! "
'Twas then she burst, to prove me wrong,
Into a sudden storm of song ;
So very loud and earnest I
Feared she would break her heart and die.
" Nay, nay," I laughed, " be you no thing
To run unheard, sweet scold, but sing !
O I could hear your voice near me,
Above the din in that oak tree,
When almost all the twigs on top
Had starlings chattering without stop."

ROBIN REDBREAST

Robin on a leafless bough,
   Lord in Heaven, how he sings!
Now cold Winter's cruel Wind
   Makes playmates of withered things.

How he sings for joy this morn!
   How his breast doth pant and glow!
Look you how he stands and sings,
   Half-way up his legs in snow!

If these crumbs of bread were pearls,
   And I had no bread at home,
He should have them for that song;
   Pretty Robin Redbreast, Come.

THE TEMPER OF A MAID

The Swallow dives in yonder air,
The Robin sings with sweetest ease,
The Apple shines among the leaves,
The Leaf is dancing in the breeze ;
The Butterfly's on a warm stone,
The Bee is suckled by a flower ;
The Wasp's inside a ripe red plum,
The Ant has found his load this hour ;
The Squirrel counts and hides his nuts,
The Stoat is on a scent that burns ;
The Mouse is nibbling a young shoot,
The Rabbit sits beside his ferns ;
The Snake has found a sunny spot,
The Frog and Snail a slimy shade ;
But I can find no joy on earth,
All through the temper of a maid.

THE RAIN

I hear leaves drinking Rain ;
   I hear rich leaves on top
Giving the poor beneath
   Drop after drop ;
'Tis a sweet noise to hear
These green leaves drinking near.

And when the Sun comes out,
   After this Rain shall stop,
A wondrous Light will fill
   Each dark, round drop ;
I hope the Sun shines bright ;
   'Twill be a lovely sight.

IN MAY

Yes, I will spend the livelong day
With Nature in this month of May;
And sit beneath the trees, and share
My bread with birds whose homes are there;
While cows lie down to eat, and sheep
Stand to their necks in grass so deep;
While birds do sing with all their might,
As though they felt the earth in flight.
This is the hour I dreamed of, when
I sat surrounded by poor men;
And thought of how the Arab sat
Alone at evening, gazing at
The stars that bubbled in clear skies;

And of young dreamers when their eyes
Enjoyed methought a precious boon
In the adventures of the Moon
Whose light, behind the Cloud's dark bars,
Searched for her stolen flocks of stars.
When I, hemmed in by wrecks of men,
Thought of some lonely cottage then,
Full of sweet books; and miles of sea
With passing ships, in front of me;
And having, on the other hand,
A flowery, green, bird-singing land.

AUTUMN

Autumn grows old; he, like some
  simple one,
    In Summer's castaways is strangely
      clad;
Such withered things the winds in frolic mad
Shake from his feeble hand and forehead wan.

Autumn is sighing for his early gold,
  And in his tremble dropping his remains;
  The brook talks more, as one bereft of brains,
Who singeth loud, delirious with the cold.

O now with drowsy June one hour to be!
  Scarce waking strength to hear the hum of bees,
  Or cattle lowing under shady trees,
Knee-deep in waters loitering to the sea.

I would that drowsy June awhile were here,
  The amorous South wind carrying all the vale—
  Save that white lily true to star as pale,
Whose secret day dream Phoebus burns to hear.

RAPTURES

Sing for the sun your lyric, lark,
    Of twice ten thousand notes ;
Sing for the moon, you nightingales,
    Whose light shall kiss your throats ;
Sing, sparrows, for the soft warm rain,
    To wet your feathers through ;
And, when a rainbow's in the sky,
    Sing you, cuckoo—"Cuckoo!"

Sing for your five blue eggs, fond thrush,
    By many a leaf concealed ;
You starlings, wrens, and blackbirds sing
    In every wood and field :
While I, who failed to give my love
    Long raptures twice as fine,
Will for her beauty breathe this one—
    A sigh, that's more divine.

EASTER

What exultations in my mind
From the love-bite of this Easter wind !
My head thrown back, my face doth shine
Like yonder Sun's but warmer mine.
A butterfly—from who knows where ?—
Comes with a stagger through the air,
And, lying down, doth ope and close
His wings as babies work their toes :
Perhaps he thinks of pressing tight
Into his wings a little light !
And many a bird hops in between
The leaves he dreams of, long and green,
And sings for nipple-buds that show
Where the full-breasted leaves must grow.
Winter is dead, and now we sing
This welcome to the new-born Spring.

CHARMS

She walks as lightly as the fly
Skates on the water in July.

To hear her moving petticoat,
For me is music's highest note.

Stones are not heard, when her
feet pass,
No more than tumps of moss
or grass.

When she is still, she's like the flower,
To be a butterfly next hour.

The brook laughs not more sweet, when he
Trips over pebbles suddenly.

My Love, like him, can whisper low—
When he comes where green cresses grow.

She rises like the lark, that hour
He goes halfway to meet a shower.

A fresher drink is in her looks
Than Nature gives me, or old books.

THE ONE SINGER

Dead leaves from off the tree
    Make whirlpools on the ground ;
Like dogs that chase their tails,
    Those leaves go round and round ;
Like birds unfledged and young,
    The old bare branches cry ;
Branches that shake and bend
    To feel the winds go by.

No other sound is heard,
    Save from those boughs so bare—
Hark ! who sings that one song ?
    'Tis Robin sings so rare.
How sweet, like those sad tunes
    In homes where grief's not known ;
Or that a blind girl sings
    When she is left alone.

THE HOUR OF MAGIC

This is the hour of magic, when the Moon
   With her bright wand has charmed the
      tallest tree
To stand stone still with all his million leaves !
   I feel around me things I cannot see ;
I hold my breath, as nature holds her own.
   And do the mice and birds, the horse and cow,
Sleepless in this deep silence, so intense,
   Believe a miracle has happened now,
And wait to hear a sound they'll recognise,
   To prove they still have life with earthly ties ?

OH, SWEET CONTENT

Oh, sweet content, that turns the labourer's sweat
    To tears of joy, and shines the roughest face;
How often have I sought you high and low,
    And found you still in some lone quiet place.

Here, in my room, when full of happy dreams,
    With no life heard beyond that merry sound
Of moths that on my lighted ceiling kiss
    Their shadows as they dance and dance around.

Or in a garden, on a summer's night,
    When I have seen the dark and solemn air
Blink with the blind bat's wings, and heaven's
        bright face
    Twitch with the stars that shine in thousands
    there.

ANGRY

My love sits angry; see!
Her foot shakes in the light;
Her timid, little foot,
That else would hide from sight.

Her left hand props her cheek;
Its little finger plays
Upon her under-lip,
And makes a harp-like noise.

Her lip's red manuscript
She has unrolled and spread;
So I may read ill news,
And hang my guilty head.

My love sits angry; see!
She's red up to her eyes;
And was her face flogged by
The wings of Butterflies?

Her right hand's in her lap,
So small, so soft, so white;
She in her anger makes
Five fingers hide from sight.

Two golden curls have now
Dropped out of their silk net;
There they must stop, for she
Will not restore them yet.

My love, she is so fair
When in this angry way,
That did she guess my thoughts,
She'd quarrel every day.

APRIL'S BOYS AND GIRLS

Of primrose boys
 April has many ;
He seems as fond
 Of them as any ;
He shows the world
Those boys in gold.

But violets are
 His girls, whom he
Shuts up in some
 Green nunnery ;
So does he prove
His deepest love.

April, a girl
 Of yours is found ;
High walls of grass
 Hemmed her around :
April, forgive me—
I followed a bee.

THE OX

Why should I pause, poor beast, to praise
    Thy back so red, thy sides so white;
And on thy brow those curls in which
    Thy mournful eyes take no delight?

I dare not make fast friends with kine,
    Nor sheep nor fowl that cannot fly;
For they live not for Nature's voice,
    Since 'tis man's will when they must die.

So if I call thee some pet name,
    And give thee of my care to-day,
Where wilt thou be to-morrow morn
    When I turn curious eyes thy way?

Nay, I'll not miss what I'll not find,
    And I'll find no fond cares for thee ;
So take away those great sad eyes
    That stare across yon fence at me.

See you that Robin by himself,
    Perched on that leafless apple branch ;
His breast like one red apple left—
    The last and best of all—by chance ?

If I do but give heed to him,
    He will come daily to my door ;
And 'tis the will of God, not man,
    When Robin Redbreast comes no more.

SEEKING JOY

Joy, how I sought thee !
  Silver I spent, and gold,
On the pleasures of this world,
  In splendid garments clad ;
The wine I drank was sweet,
  Rich morsels I did eat—
Oh, but my life was sad !
  Joy, how I sought thee !

Joy, I have found thee !
  Far from the halls of Mirth,
Back to the soft green earth,
  Where people are not many ;
I find thee, Joy, in hours
  With clouds, and birds and flowers—
Thou dost not charge one penny.
  Joy, I have found thee !

THE RAINBOW

Rainbows are lovely things :
   The bird, that shakes a cold, wet wing,
Chatters with ecstasy,
   But has no breath to sing :
No wonder, when the air
Has a double-rainbow there !

Look, there's a rainbow now !
   See how that lovely rainbow throws
Her jewelled arm around
   This world, when the rain goes !
And how I wish the rain
Would come again, and again !

THE SLUGGARD

A jar of cider and my pipe,
  In summer, under shady tree;
A book of one that made his mind
  Live by its sweet simplicity:
Then must I laugh at kings who sit
  In richest chambers, signing scrolls;
And princes cheered in public ways,
  And stared at by a thousand fools.

Let me be free to wear my dreams,
  Like weeds in some mad maiden's hair,
When she believes the earth has not
  Another maid so rich and fair;
And proudly smiles on rich and poor,
  The queen of all fair women then:
So I, dressed in my idle dreams,
  Will think myself the king of men.

THE MOON

Thy beauty haunts me, heart and soul,
  Oh thou fair Moon, so close and bright ;
Thy beauty makes me like the child,
  That cries aloud to own thy light :
The little child that lifts each arm,
To press thee to her bosom warm.

Though there are birds that sing this night
  With thy white beams across their throats,
Let my deep silence speak for me
  More than for them their sweetest notes :
Who worships thee till music fails
Is greater than thy nightingales.

THE VILLAIN

While joy gave clouds the light of stars,
  That beamed where'er they looked ;
And calves and lambs had tottering knees,
  Excited, while they sucked ;
While every bird enjoyed his song,
  Without one thought of harm or wrong—
I turned my head and saw the wind,
  Not far from where I stood,
Dragging the corn by her golden hair,
  Into a dark and lonely wood.

YOUNG BEAUTY

When at each door the ruffian winds
    Have laid a dying man to groan,
And filled the air on winter nights
    With cries of infants left alone ;
And every thing that has a bed
    Will sigh for others that have none :

On such a night, when bitter cold,
    Young Beauty, full of love thoughts sweet,
Can redden in her looking-glass ;
    With but one gown on, in bare feet,
She from her own reflected charms
    Can feel the joy of summer's heat.

LOVE'S CAUTION

Tell them, when you are home again
  How warm the air was now ;
How silent were the birds and leaves,
  And of the moon's full glow ;
And how we saw afar
  A falling star :
It was a tear of pure delight
  Ran down the face of Heaven this happy night.

Our kisses are but love in flower,
  Until that greater time
When, gathering strength, those flowers take wing,
  And Love can reach his prime.
And now, my heart's delight,
  Good night, Good night ;
Give me the last sweet kiss—
  But do not breathe at home one word of this !

THE CAPTIVE LION

Thou that in fury with thy knotted tail
　　Hast made this iron floor thy beaten drum ;
That now in silence walks thy little space—
　　Like a sea captain—careless what may come :

What power has brought your majesty to this,
　　Who gave those eyes their dull and sleepy look ;
Who took their lightning out, and from thy throat
　　The thunder when the whole wide forest shook ?

It was that man who went again, alone,
　　Into thy forest dark—Lord, he was brave !
That man a fly has killed, whose bones are left
　　Unburied till an earthquake digs his grave.

THE MASK

When I complained of April's day,
  Her silent birds, her absent Sun ;
And how her mist but added tears
  Unto the dew's, that had not gone—

Young April heard and, suddenly,
  Came leaping from her strange disguise ;
Off came her dark-November mask,
  And showed the world her laughing eyes.

THE HAPPY CHILD

I saw this day sweet flowers grow thick—
But not one like the child did pick.

I heard the packhounds in green park—
But no dog like the child heard bark.

I heard this day bird after bird—
But not one like the child has heard.

A hundred butterflies saw I—
But not one like the child saw fly.

I saw the horses roll in grass—
But no horse like the child saw pass.

My world this day has lovely been—
But not like what the child has seen.

LEISURE

What is this life if, full of care,
We have no time to stand and stare.

No time to stand beneath the boughs
And stare as long as sheep or cows.

No time to see, when woods we pass,
Where squirrels hide their nuts in grass.

No time to see, in broad daylight,
Streams full of stars, like stars at night.

No time to turn at Beauty's glance,
And watch her feet, how they can dance.

No time to wait till her mouth can
Enrich that smile her eyes began.

A poor life this if, full of care,
We have no time to stand and stare.

A BLIND CHILD

Her baby brother laughed last night,
   The blind child asked her mother why ;
   It was the light that caught his eye.
Would she might laugh to see that light !

The presence of a stiffened corse
   Is sad enough ; but, to my mind,
   The presence of a child that's blind,
In a green garden, is far worse.

She felt my cloth—for worldly place ;
   She felt my face—if I was good ;
   My face lost more than half its blood,
For fear her hand would wrongly trace.

We're in the garden, where are bees
   And flowers, and birds, and butterflies ;
   One greedy fledgling runs and cries
For all the food his parent sees !

I see them all : flowers of all kind,
   The sheep and cattle on the leas ;
   The houses up the hills, the trees—
But I am dumb, for she is blind.

SWEET YOUTH

And art thou gone, sweet Youth ?   Say nay !
   For thou dost know what power was thine,
That thou couldst give vain shadows flesh,
   And laughter without any wine,
From the heart fresh.

And art thou gone, sweet Youth ?   Say Nay !
   Not left me to Time's cruel spite :
He'll pull my teeth out one by one,
   He'll paint my hair first grey, then white,
He'll scrape my bone.

And art thou gone, sweet youth ?   Alas !
   For ever gone !   I know it well :
Earth has no atom, nor the sky,
   That has not thrown the kiss Farewell—
Sweet youth, Good-Bye !

ADVICE

Now, you two eyes, that have all night been sleeping,
Come into the meadows, where the lambs are leaping ;
See how they start at every swallow's shadow
That darts across their faces and their meadow.
See how the blades spring upright, when the sun
Takes off the weight of raindrops, one by one.
See how a shower, that freshened leaves of grass,
Can make that bird's voice fresher than it was.
See how the squirrels lash the quiet trees
Into a tempest, where there is no breeze !
Now, you two eyes, that have all night been sleeping,
Come into the meadows, where the lambs are leaping.

THE OWL

he boding Owl, that in despair
     Doth moan and shiver on
          warm nights—
Shall that bird prophesy for me
     The fall of heaven's eternal
          lights ?

When in the thistled field of Age
     I take my final walk on earth,
     Still will I make that Owl's despair
A thing to fill my heart with mirth.

THE CAT

Within this porch, across the way,
*   I see two naked eyes this night;*
Two eyes that neither shut nor blink,
*   Searching my face with a green light.*

But cats to me are strange, so strange—
*   I cannot sleep if one is near;*
And though I'm sure I see those eyes,
*   I'm not so sure a body's there!*

IN DAYS GONE

I had a sweet companion once,
    And in the meadows we did roam ;
And in the one-star night returned
    Together home.

When Bees did roar like midget bulls,
    Or quietly rob nodding Flowers—
We two did roam the fields so green,
    In Summer hours.

She like the Rill did laugh, when he
    Plays in the quiet woods alone ;
She was as red as Summer's rose—
    The first one blown.

Her hair as soft as any moss
    That running water still keeps wet ;
And her blue eye—it seemed as if
    A Violet

Had in a Lily's centre grown,
    To see the blue, and white around—
'Twas tender as the Glowworm's light
    On a lost mound.

And, like the face of a sweet well
    Buried alive in a stone place—
So calm, so fresh, so soft, so bright
    Was that child's face.

A GREAT TIME

Sweet Chance, that led my steps abroad,
    Beyond the town, where wildflowers grow,
A rainbow and a cuckoo, Lord,
    How rich and great the times are now !
        Know, all ye sheep
        And cows, that keep
On staring that I stand so long
    In grass that's wet from heavy rain—
A rainbow and a cuckoo's song
    May never come together again ;
        May never come
        This side the tomb.

THE RAT

"That woman there is almost dead,
  Her feet and hands like heavy lead;
  Her cat's gone out for his delight,
  He will not come again this night.

"Her husband in a pothouse drinks,
  Her daughter at a soldier winks;
  Her son is at his greatest game,
  Teasing the cobbler old and lame.

"Now with these teeth that powder stones,
  I'll pick at one of her cheek bones:
  When husband, son and daughter come,
  They'll soon see who was left at home."

THE HERMIT

What moves that lonely man is not the boom
  Of waves that beat against the cliff so strong ;
Nor roar of thunder, when that travelling voice
  Is caught by rocks that carry far along.

'Tis not the groan of oak tree in its prime,
  When lightning strikes its solid heart to dust ;
Nor frozen pond when, melted by the sun,
  It suddenly doth break its sparkling crust.

What moves that man is when the blind bat taps
  His window when he sits alone at night ;
Or when the small bird sounds like some great beast
  Among the dead dry leaves so frail and light.

Or when the moths on his night-pillow beat
  Such heavy blows he fears they'll break his bones ;
Or when a mouse inside the papered walls
  Comes like a tiger crunching through the stones.

IMPUDENCE

One morning, when the world was grey and cold,
  And every face looked dull and full of care,
There passed me, puffing clouds of silver breath,
  A lovely maiden, with a jaunty air.

The red carnations flamed in both her cheeks,
  Her teeth all there and shown ; while either eye
Shone like a little pool on Christchurch Hill
  When it has stolen more than half the sky.

And when I saw such beauty, young and fresh,
  So proud, although the day was grey and cold,
"Who ever saw" I laughed, and stared amazed,
  "Such impudence before this old world !"

WINTER'S BEAUTY

Is it not fine to walk in spring,
When leaves are born, and hear birds sing ?
And when they lose their singing powers,
In summer, watch the bees at flowers ?
Is it not fine, when summer's past,
To have the leaves, no longer fast,
Biting my heel where'er I go,
Or dancing lightly on my toe ?
Now winter's here and rivers freeze,
As I walk out I see the trees,
Wherein the pretty squirrels sleep,
All standing in the snow so deep :
And every twig, however small,
Is blossomed white and beautiful.
Then welcome, winter, with thy power
To make this tree a big white flower ;
To make this tree a lovely sight,
With fifty brown arms draped in white,
While thousands of small fingers show
In soft white gloves of purest snow.

IN THE SNOW

Hear how my friend the robin sings!
That little hunchback in the snow,
As it comes down as fast as rain.
The air is cold, the wind doth blow,
And still his heart can feel no pain.

And I with heart as light as his,
And to my ankles deep in snow,
Hold up a fist as cold as death's;
And into it I laugh and blow—
I laugh and blow my life's warm breath.

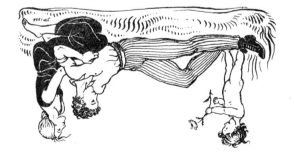

A LIFE'S LOVE

How I do love to sit and dream
Of that sweet passion, when I meet
The lady I must love for life!
The very thought makes my Soul beat
It's wings, as though it saw that light
Silver the rims of my black night.

I see her bring a crimson mouth
To open at a kiss and close;
I see her bring her two fair cheeks,
That I may paint on each a rose;
I see her two hands, like doves white,
Fly into mine and hide from sight.

In fancy hear her soft, sweet voice;
My eager soul, to catch her words,
Waits at the ear, with Noah's haste
To take God's message-bearing birds;
What passion she will in me move—
The lady I for life must love!

A SWALLOW THAT FLEW INTO THE ROOM

I give thee back thy freedom, bird,
But know, I am amazed to see
These lovely feathers, which thou hast
Concealed so many years from me.

Oft have I watched thee cut the name
Of Summer in the clear, blue air,
And praised thy skilful lettering—
But never guessed thou wert so fair.

It is, maybe, thou hast no wish
For praise save for thy works of grace;
Thou scornest beauty, like the best
And wisest of our human race.

A WINTER'S NIGHT

I t is a winter's night and cold,
The wind is blowing half a gale;
I, with my red-hot poker, stir
To take the chill off my
old ale.

I drink my ale, I smoke my pipe,
While fire-flames leap to light the cold;
And yet, before my bedtime comes
I must look out on the wide world.

And what strange beauty I behold:
The wild fast-driven clouds this night
Hurled at the moon, whose smiling face
Still shines with undiminished light.

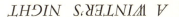

RAGS AND BONES

This morning, as I wandered forth,
I heard a man cry, "Rags and Bones !"
And little children in the streets
Went home for bottles, bones and rags,
To barter for his toys and sweets.

And then I thought of grown-up man,
That in our dreams we trust a God
Will think our rags and bones a boon,
And give us His immortal sweets
For these poor lives cast off so soon.

The mind, they say, will gather strength
That broods on what is hard to know :
The fear of unfamiliar things
Is better than their parents' love
To teach young birds to use their wings.

But riddles are not made for me,
My joy's in beauty, not its cause :
Then give me but the open skies,
And birds that sing in a green wood
That's snow-bound by anemones.